Active Imagination Activity Book

50 Sensorimotor Activities to Improve Focus, Attention, Strength & Coordination

Active Imagination Activity Book: 50 Sensorimotor Activities to Improve Focus, Attention, Strength, & Coordination
by Kelly Tilley

All marketing and publishing rights guaranteed to and reserved by:

(817) 303-1516
(817) 277-2270 (fax)

E-mail: info@sensoryworld.com
www.sensoryworld.com

Book design ©Sensory World
Cover by John Yacio III; Interior by Cindy Williams

ISBN: 9781935567288

Table of Contents

Introduction

Childhood is a time filled with new motor challenges and all kinds of hurdles. Kids are busy learning to tie their shoes, zip their jackets, ride a bicycle, negotiate the playground, and write their names. All of these skills require strength, coordination, and the ability to focus and attend.

The activities in this book tap into what kids love best—play. This is a compilation of fun, easy, and imaginative exercises to build skills necessary for your child to meet the challenges of everyday life at home, at school, and out in the community.

Whether your child or client can benefit from movement activities that are calming, energizing, or strengthening, or from getting exercise in general, you will find this book to be a helpful resource at home, at school, or in a therapeutic setting. The large, clear pictures and concise descriptions are especially helpful for children who have difficulties with language, cognition, or attention. The activities themselves require little or no equipment, and the duration of the activities can

be easily adapted as the child's abilities advance. Every illustration and description helps the child to imagine being a particular animal or insect (eg, "Armadillo Roll-Up" and "Walking Stick"), and, in some cases, describes how to move through some adventurous terrain (eg, "Thin Ice," "Moving Mountains," and "Canoeing Down the River"). Active Imagination sensorimotor activities are unique because they are not simply a set of exercises. They inspire the child to use his imagination and participate in a meaningful and inspirational way. Children who have done these activities report that they enjoy pretending to be various animals and insects. Additionally, children want to participate in these sensorimotor activities longer than in traditional exercises (sit-ups, push-ups, etc). Under the guidance of a parent, teacher, or therapist, children will enjoy using their imaginations while engaging in fun and playful activities designed to help improve their core strength, upper-body strength and stability, sensory regulation (their ability to calm or energize their systems), and their overall functioning.

Highlights of Active Imagination Activities

- 50 Uniquely illustrated, fun, and easy activities to help your child improve strength, coordination, focus, and attention.

- Tabs along the border of each page help the parent, teacher, or therapist identify whether the activity will help build core strength or upper-extremity strength or whether the activity is calming or energizing.

- The quick-reference chart lists the activities and the corresponding areas that are addressed in each case.

- Most activities require no equipment. A small or medium-sized exercise ball is necessary for some activities. Most other equipment can be found in the home or in the clinic (eg, pillows, cushions, blankets, and a chair or bench).

- If you have concerns about your child's abilities, it is recommended that you consult an occupational therapist regarding activities to improve function, learning, and behavior.

- For parents, a helpful way to use this book is to select two or three activities to do with your child before and after school. Calming activities may be helpful for a bedtime routine or prior to doing homework. For teachers, this book can help provide fun movement breaks for the whole class. Upper-extremity strengthening activities are great preparation for handwriting. For therapists, this book can help streamline sensory diets and increase the follow-through with home programming. These activities are also fun to do as part of obstacle courses, treasure hunts, and group activities.

Selecting Activities for Each Child: Description of Tabs

Tabs along the bottom border of each page allow the teacher, parent, or therapist to select activities that are ideal for calming, energizing, upper-extremity strengthening, and core strengthening. The tabs allow daily routines of activities to be developed easily. Tabs also make it easier to select activities that are specific to the child's area(s) of need. Often, these sensorimotor activities improve more than one area, so multiple tabs will reflect this along the bottom of the page. For example, "Meteorite Launch" is an energizing and core-strengthening activity.

Every child has a unique set of sensory needs and abilities. Some children appear overly aroused (too wired, unable to sit still), while others appear underaroused (too sluggish, have trouble getting moving). Improving children's level of arousal and their ability to attend and focus can be achieved through sensorimotor activity.

Energizing Activities

Activities that are designated as "energizing" provide input to the body that "revs" up or "perks" up the nervous system. The movements are usually quick and often involve changes in head position. These activities typically involve jumping, rolling, bending forward, and leaping over objects.

Upper-Body Strengthening Activities

Activities that are designated as "upper-body strengthening" involve bearing one's weight on extended arms and doing modified push-ups, animal walks, and the like. These activities all help to build the child's strength and stability in the shoulder girdle, arms, wrists, hands, and fingers. Upper-body strength is critical for the development of fine-motor coordination, which is necessary for children to perform everyday tasks such as writing, buttoning, zipping, and tying their shoes.

Core-Strengthening Activities

Activities designated as "core strengthening" target the large muscle groups of the hips, trunk, and shoulder girdle. These activities build postural control, bilateral coordination, balance, and the ability to grade movements. Climbing, running, jumping, and playing on the playground are accomplished more easily with good core strength. Development of the core is also important for regulation and attention. Activities that require stability and postural control, such as sitting at a school desk during the day, are also achieved more easily when the child has better core strength.

Calming Activities

Activities that are designated as "calming" provide input to muscles and joints in a slow and/or rhythmic way. These activities generally focus on deep pressure and "heavy work." Deep-pressure activities refer to input such as squishing your body under cushions or being rolled up snugly in a blanket. "Heavy work" refers to any movement activity performed against resistance (pushing heavy objects or pushing up against gravity).

Note: Calming activities are great preparation for bedtime. They are also helpful prior to tabletop work at school or before doing homework.

The Road Roller

Time to flatten out that bumpy road. Start in "push-up" position with your feet on a large ball. Slowly roll the ball toward your hands by tucking your legs up to your tummy. Slowly return to starting position by straightening your legs. Your hands should stay flat on the floor.

1

Upper-Body Strengthening   Core Strengthening   Calming

Hot Dog

Lay a heavy blanket on the floor. Lie at one end of the blanket and have someone roll it up snugly against you so you become a hot dog in a bun. She can pretend to slather on some mustard and ketchup by pressing firmly down the length of the blanket.

Be careful, someone might try to eat you!

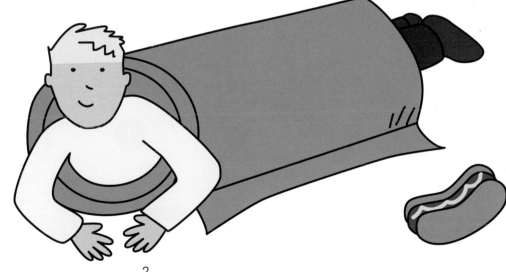

2

Fishing Pole

Start by lying over a large ball on your tummy. Walk your hands forward until only your legs are supported by the ball. Lower your head down to the ground by bending your arms, then slowly raise your head back up by straightening your arms. Keep your body straight, like a fishing pole.

FISH ON!

3

Upper-Body Strengthening   Core Strengthening   Calming

Dolphin Dive

Start with your hands on the floor and your arms and legs out straight. Slowly "dive" into the water by lowering your hips toward the floor. Pause for a few seconds when you get to a "push-up" position and your body is in a straight line.

Now, lower yourself slowly into the ocean by bending your arms and keeping your body straight, until you are resting on the floor.

AHH. FEEL THE *COOL OCEAN WATER*!

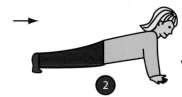

1

2

3

Upper-Body Strengthening   Core Strengthening   Calming

Pizza

Lie flat on the floor on your tummy, like you're pizza dough lying on the countertop. Have another person use a large ball to roll out the "pizza dough" by pushing downward on the ball as she rolls it back and forth over your body.

Have her pile on cushions and pillows to be the "toppings" on the pizza—sauce, cheese, and pepperoni.

MAMMA MIA! YUMMY!

Hippo's Hungry

Munch, munch, this hippo is rolling back and forth to get lunch.

Place a pile of beanbags, rolled-up socks, or small toys in front of a large ball. Push forward off your feet to roll over the ball on your tummy. Stop yourself by extending your arms and placing your hands on the floor. Grab one beanbag and push yourself backward over the ball. Place the beanbag behind the ball. Repeat.

This is fun to do as a race to see which hippo can "eat" the most beanbags!

Upper-Body Strengthening   **Core Strengthening**   **Calming**

Moving Mountains

Stand in front of a wall, with the wall at about arms' length. Use both hands to push as hard as you can against the wall, pretending to move a gigantic mountain. Push it for several seconds. Good job! I think it moved!

Upper-Body Strengthening

Calming

Desert Lizard

The sand is HOT! The lizard cools off his feet by lifting them up one at a time off the hot ground.

Start in "push-up" position. Lift your right arm up for several seconds, then your left arm. Try lifting your right leg and then your left leg. It can be tricky!

Upper-Body Strengthening   **Core Strengthening**   **Calming**

Bird's Nest

Hide several toys ("eggs") under a big pile of cushions, pillows, and blankets (your "nest"). Then dig out the toys one at a time. Help to clean up the "nest" when you're done. Tweet tweet!

Calming

Roly-Poly Bug

Start by lying over a large ball on your tummy. Roll back and forth over the ball, alternately pushing off your hands and then your feet like a roly-poly bug.

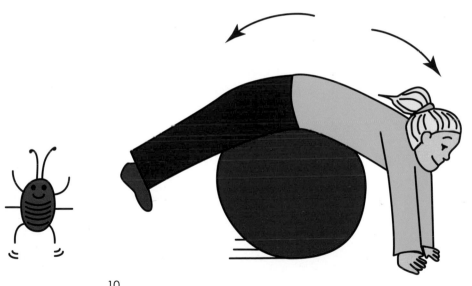

Upper-Body Strengthening   Core Strengthening   Calming

The Bulldozer

Time for some construction-site cleanup!

Fill a laundry basket or box with toys, books, and/or blocks. Using two hands, push the box across the room like a bulldozer. Don't forget to unload the basket when you are done!

11

The Praying Mantis

The praying mantis is an insect that holds its body very still so it can stalk its prey without being seen.

Start in a half-kneeling position (with one knee down and one knee up). Stretch your arms out straight at your sides. Hold this position as if you were a praying mantis. See how many beanbags can be placed on your arms, head, and knee before they fall off!

Core Strengthening

Calming

The Walking Stick

This insect is a mimic—he can pretend to be a twig on a tree.

Hold your body in tightly and stretch out to make yourself really long, to be the longest walking stick around. Then get onto your hands and knees on the floor. Extend your right arm out straight in front of you, and extend your left leg out behind you until it is level with your back. Hold this position for several seconds, then switch to the opposite arm and leg.

Upper-Body Strengthening   Core Strengthening   Calming

Rock, Paper, Scissors

First, be a rock by tucking yourself up into a ball while crouching on the floor. Then, be paper by lying flat on the floor on your tummy and stretching your arms out. Finally, be scissors by scrambling up off the floor into a standing position, with your legs apart and your hands on your head to form the handles of your scissors!

Try to move between these positions quickly. Have someone yell out different positions in a different order, or play with a friend and see who wins—rock beats scissors, scissors beat paper, and paper beats rock.

14

Bunny Rabbit

Be a furry little bunny, looking for some carrots!

While keeping your feet together, hop around the room to pick up some "carrots" (beanbags, rolled-up socks, or small toys). Gather them up in a basket or box.

15

Cotton Candy

Swirl pink fluffy sugar into cotton candy for a sweet treat!!

With your hands on your head and your feet together, jump up and twist to the right, so you're facing the opposite direction when you land. Repeat four more times. Then, jump and twist to the left, and repeat!

16

Grasshopper

HOP! HOP! HOP!

Start in a tucked position on the floor. Your knees stay together during this activity. Jump your feet backward into a "push-up" position, then jump them back up toward your hands.

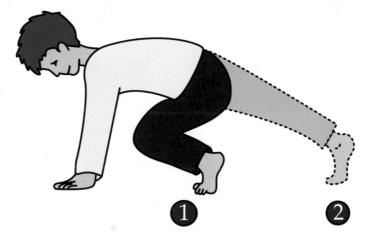

Energizing   Upper-Body Strengthening   Core Strengthening

Meteorite Launch
BLAST OFF!

Start by sitting on the floor. Then, lean back until you are propped on your elbows. Bring your knees up toward your chest. Your feet should be aimed at a person across from you who will throw a ball. Then, when he or she throws the ball at your feet, extend your legs quickly, using both feet to shoot the ball into the air like a meteorite!

Energizing

Core Strengthening

Armadillo Roll-Up

The armadillo curls up its body to protect it from predators. I think a large bear is coming—let's roll up!

Lie on the floor on your back. Stretch your arms over your head. Then, bring your arms up over your head as you sit up and tuck your legs in. Tuck yourself into a ball and balance only on your bottom for several seconds. Phew! You're safe from the bear!

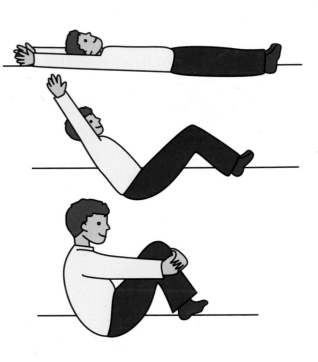

19

Swimming

It's time for a dip in the pool!

Lie on your tummy. With your arms and legs out straight, pump them up and down, alternating right and left, while keeping them off the floor. Do this for 5 to 10 seconds.

Then, lie on your back and pretend to do the backstroke by making a circular motion with your arms and kicking your legs up and down above the floor.

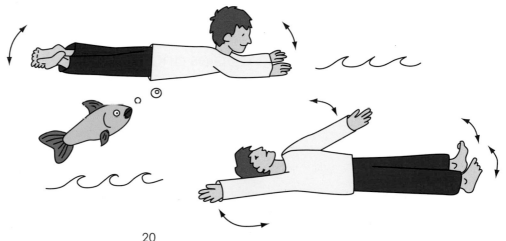

20

Apple-Picking

Mmm—crisp, juicy apples.

Cut out some paper circles to be your apples. Use tape to stick them onto the "tree" (your mom or dad, or even your brother!). Then, jump up to pluck one apple at a time off the tree. You could put letters or numbers on the apples and try to pick certain ones as they're called out.

The Windmill

Start with your legs apart and your arms straight above your head, with your palms together. Now, keeping your arms straight and your hands together, move your body in a large circle, going to the side, to the floor, to the other side, and back up again like a windmill.

Keep those arms straight as you sweep down to the floor and then high above your head. Then, reverse the direction of the windmill.

WHOOOOSH...

22

Thin Ice

Set up a path of cushions and pillows across a room.
Walk across the wobbly "ice" to get to safety.
Try not to step in the freezing cold water!

BRRRR!

Alligator Legs

Chomp your legs together—bite, bite!

Start by bending forward with your hands on a low bench or chair. Spread your feet wide apart, then do a little jump as you snap your feet together like an alligator's jaws! Then, jump your feet back out again. Keep your arms straight while you are chomping your legs together and apart. Chomp!

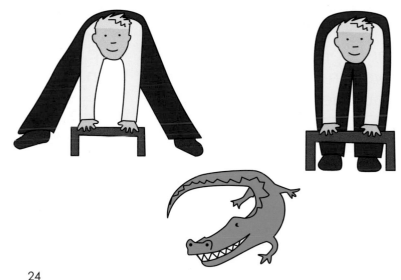

Energizing   **Upper-Body Strengthening**   **Core Strengthening**

Lava Leaps

Oh no, the volcano has erupted! Time to jump over the lava flow.

Run several feet and leap over an imaginary hot lava flow. Run back the opposite direction and leap over the flow again. Don't burn your toes! Yeow!

25

Ski Patrol

Ski down the mountain to get to the lodge at the bottom. Lay down a jump rope or draw a long chalk line. Now jump from side to side like a skier, all the way down the length of the rope, while keeping your feet together.

WHEE!

Ladybug Hop

Start in a standing position. Then jump up, tucking your knees up to your chest, and land on your feet again!

27

Catching Flies

The frog jumps up to catch some flies!

Put some rubber bugs or beanbags on the floor. Squat down to pick up a bug or beanbag, then jump back up into the air, straightening your arms and legs. Squat back down on the floor when you land and grab another bug. Yummy!

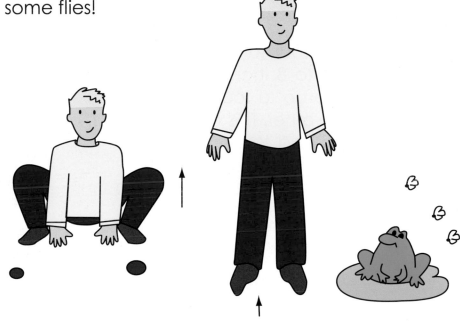

28

Reach for the Stars!

YOU CAN DO IT!

An adult will stick four to six stars on the wall about 4 to 8 inches above your reach. Jump up to touch each star, one after the other. This way, you have to jump up and to the right or left to touch the stars! When you're done going one way, jump back the other way to touch all the stars again. Success!

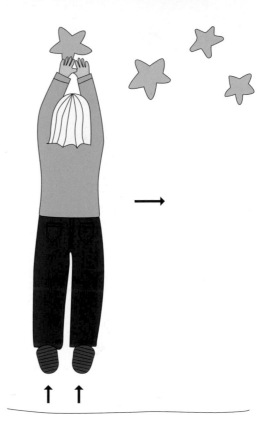

The Inchworm

Get into a "push-up" position. Your body and arms should be straight. Keeping your hands in place on the floor, hop both feet forward as close to your hands as possible, so your body is now in a tucked position. Now, slowly walk your hands forward, gradually stretching out your body until you return to the original "push-up" position.

Measure the room with "inchworms." How many can you do before you run out of room?

Energizing   **Upper-Body Strengthening**   **Core Strengthening**

Banana Split

Yum. Change from a banana into the cherry on top!

While lying on the floor, be the banana by rolling from your front to your back. Then, tuck up into a small ball to be the cherry by lifting your shoulders and legs off the floor so you are balancing only on your bottom.

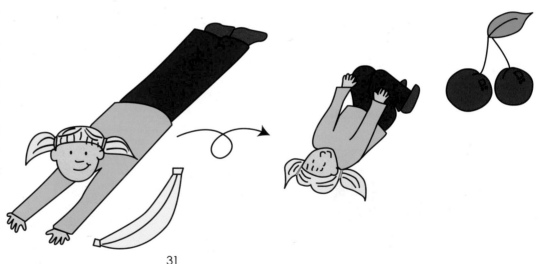

31

Bumper Ball

This is game that requires two people, but if you don't have another person to play with, you could hit the ball against a wall instead.

Lie on your tummy several feet away from your partner, who should be lying on his or her tummy facing you. Stretch your arms out straight in front of you. Now, hit a ball back and forth between you using both hands, while keeping your arms off the floor. Don't let your elbows rest on the floor!

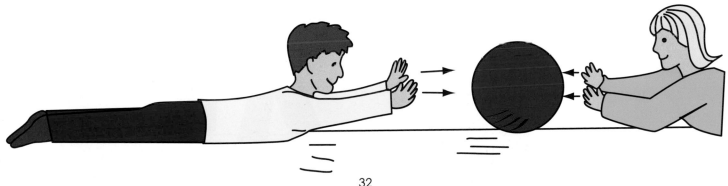

Energizing   Upper-Body Strengthening   Core Strengthening

Jack in the Box

Crouch on the floor, in a "tucked" position. Then, jump up with your arms up high ("ta-da!") and your legs apart, so you look like a star. Surprise! Jump back down to a tucked position, as if you're going back inside your "box."

33

Twinkle Toes

Start by lying on the floor on your back. Raise your legs and arms so they're pointing at the ceiling, as straight as possible. Tighten and tuck your stomach muscles to lift your shoulders off the floor, and touch your toes for 2 to 5 seconds before slowly lowering your shoulders back down to floor.

Upper-Body Strengthening

Calming

The Rattler

The rattler is a dangerous snake that has been seen by many hikers. It is known for its distinctive warning rattle when people get too close.

Lie on the floor on your tummy and "commando crawl" under chairs and tables, keeping your belly low to the floor like a rattler.

Energizing   Upper-Body Strengthening   Core Strengthening

The Log Roll

Lumberjacks and loggers often have to be very good at walking on floating logs.

While standing on a wobble board, try to catch a ball that is thrown to you from various directions. If you don't have a wobble board, you can try to keep your balance while standing on a firm cushion or pillow.

CATCH

36

Core Strengthening

Soldier-Teepee

Just like good old jumping jacks!

These are easier when you use words to visualize the shape or position you want your body to take. Stand like a soldier, with your feet together and your arms at your sides. Then, jump to make a teepee, with your feet apart and your arms above your head, palms together, forming the point of the teepee.

Teensy-Weensy Spider

Take off your shoes and socks. Get down on all fours, about a foot from a wall, with your feet closest to the wall. Take two or three steps up the wall with your bare feet, with your arms extended and your hands firmly on the floor.

Hold this position for 4 or 5 seconds before slowly walking your feet back down the wall to the floor.

Upper-Body Strengthening   **Core Strengthening**   **Calming**

The Bear Walk

Roar! This bear is looking for some honey.

With your arms out straight, bend forward at the waist and put your hands on the floor. Your legs should be kept as straight as possible. Now, walk on your hands and feet, like a bear lumbering through the forest. Don't forget to growl and stop for some delicious honey!

Upper-Body Strengthening   Core Strengthening

Crabby's on the Road Again

Get into a crab position, with your arms out behind your body, your knees bent, and your bottom lifted off the floor to form a "table top." Then walk across the room several yards, keeping your bottom off the floor. You could collect things along the way and try to balance them on your stomach as you creep around the room. For example, you could pick up books or toys.

40

Upper-Body Strengthening   Core Strengthening

Icy Stairs

Sometimes the only way to get down a flight of frozen steps is on your bottom! Go slowly. Start by sitting at the top of a small staircase. Use your hands to push your bottom up and then lower it down to the next step. Move your hands down one step. Repeat until you've safely reached the floor.

Upper-Body Strengthening   Core Strengthening

Daddy Longlegs

Look at those long spider legs! Lie on your back on the floor, then prop yourself up on your elbows. Using only your feet, move beanbags from the top of a bench or low table onto the floor in a slow, controlled manner. Your feet should not touch the floor.

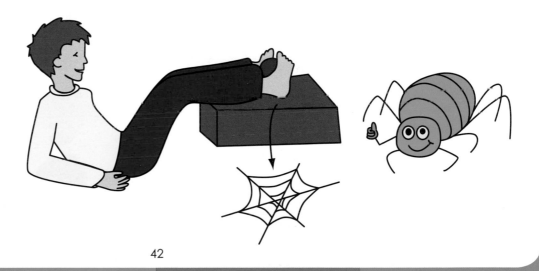

The Water Bug

Water bugs can skim over the surface of the water. Give it a try!

Start by lying on the floor on your tummy, with your arms stretched out in front of you. Bring your arms to your sides and out front again, while keeping them off the floor. Your head should be up, with your eyes looking forward.

Crabby Toss

Get into a crab position, with your arms out behind your body, your knees bent, and your bottom lifted off the floor to form a "table top." From this position, toss beanbags into a bowl at your feet by alternating your left and right hands. Take breaks as you need to!

44

Look, Ma—No Hands!

Place a bowl on a bench or chair about 2 feet in front of your chair. Sit up nice and tall and keep your hands at your sides for support. Use your feet to pick up a beanbag (or rolled-up socks) off the floor. Tighten your tummy muscles and lift your knees up to place the beanbag into the bowl.

Core Strengthening

The Seagull Soar

Position yourself near a wall so you can bend at the waist, with both your arms straight out and your palms flat against the wall. Now, from this position, with your back parallel with the floor and your left leg straight, slowly lift your right leg out behind your body.

When your leg is straight out behind you, let go of the wall and slowly bring your arms out to your sides to "soar" like a bird.

Balance in this position for several seconds before returning to the starting position. Then, repeat on your right leg.

46

Hot Lava

THE VOLCANO HAS ERUPTED!

Lie on your tummy on the floor, with your arms stretched forward. Lift your feet and hands up off the floor while keeping your arms and legs straight to avoid touching the hot lava!

Core Strengthening

The Blue Heron

The Blue Heron stands on one foot like a statue in swampy water, ready to nab an unsuspecting fish.

Place some beanbags on different surfaces within reach. Stand on one leg, and with slow, controlled movements, try to bend your knee and reach for the "fish" without putting your other foot down. Beanbags could then be thrown into a bowl or basket. When you've scooped them all up, switch legs and go "fishing" again.

48

The Seal from the Aquarium

Hang a balloon from the ceiling, or have someone hold a ball above you. Lie on your back on the floor. Keeping your legs straight, lift them up off the floor and touch your toes to the balloon or ball. Slowly lower your legs back to the floor.

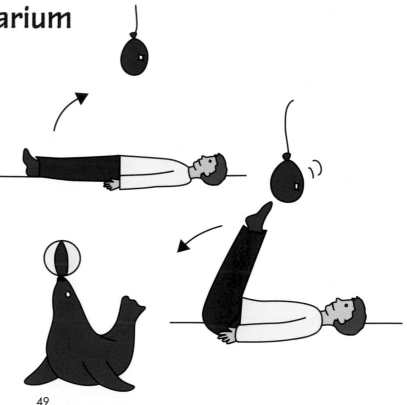

49

Canoeing Down the River

Every great outdoor adventure should start with a canoe!

Sit on the floor your with legs out straight in front of you. Use a yardstick or even a large wrapping-paper roll as a paddle. You are going to paddle on the right side, then the left, as you rotate your trunk back and forth. Keep your back straight and your head held high, so you can watch out for the rapids and waterfalls!

50

	Name of Sensorimotor Activity	Energizing	Upper-Body Strengthening	Core Strengthening	Calming
1	The Road Roller		x	x	x
2	Hot Dog				x
3	Fishing Pole		x	x	x
4	Dolphin Dive		x	x	x
5	Pizza				x
6	Hippo's Hungry		x	x	x
7	Moving Mountains		x		x
8	Desert Lizard		x	x	x
9	Bird's Nest				x
10	Roly-Poly Bug		x	x	x
11	The Bulldozer		x	x	x
12	The Praying Mantis			x	x
13	The Walking Stick		x	x	x
14	Rock, Paper, Scissors	x			
15	Bunny Rabbit	x			
16	Cotton Candy	x			
17	Grasshopper	x	x	x	
18	Meteorite Launch	x		x	
19	Armadillo Roll-Up	x		x	
20	Swimming	x		x	
21	Apple-Picking	x			
22	The Windmill	x		x	
23	Thin Ice	x			
24	Alligator Legs	x	x	x	
25	Lava Leaps	x			

26	Ski Patrol	x			
27	Ladybug Hop	x			
28	Catching Flies	x			
29	Reach for the Stars!	x			
30	The Inchworm	x	x	x	
31	Banana Split	x		x	
32	Bumper Ball	x	x	x	
33	Jack in the Box	x			
34	Twinkle Toes	x		x	
35	The Rattler	x	x	x	
36	The Log Roll	x		x	
37	Soldier-Teepee	x			
38	Teensy-Weensy Spider		x	x	x
39	The Bear Walk		x	x	
40	Crabby's on the Road		x	x	
41	Icy Stairs		x	x	
42	Daddy Longlegs			x	
43	The Water Bug			x	
44	Crabby Toss			x	
45	Look, Ma—No Hands!			x	
46	The Seagull Soar			x	
47	Hot Lava			x	
48	The Blue Heron			x	
49	The Seal from the Aquarium			x	
50	Canoeing Down the River			x	

Meet the Author

Originally from Canada, Kelly Tilley, MCISc, OTR/L, is an occupational therapist at a pediatric clinic in the Chicago area. She has happily spent the past

10 years jumping, squishing, rolling, and swinging around with her clients to address their sensory needs. Her own two children and her clients are the inspiration for the activities and illustrations in this book. Kelly continues to explore new ways to provide parents, teachers, and other clinicians with fun and imaginative ways to build sensorimotor play into a child's daily routine.

ADDITIONAL RESOURCES

Picky, Picky Pete
A Boy and His Sensory Challenges
by Michelle Griffin, OT

Sensitive Sam
Sam's Sensory Adventure Has A Happy Ending!
by Marla Roth-Fisch

Special People, Special Ways
by Arlene Maguire

Squirmy Wormy
How I Learned to Help Myself
by Lynda Farrington Wilson

The Goodenoughs Get in Sync
5 Family Members Overcome Their Special Sensory Issues
by Carol Kranowitz

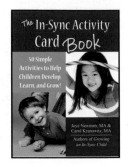

The In-Sync Activity Card Book
50 Simple Activities to Help Children Develop, Learn, and Grow!
Joye Newman, MA, and Carol Kranowitz, MA

Building Sensory Friendly Classrooms
to Support Children with Challenging Behaviors
by Rebecca Moyes

Sensory Parenting: From Newborns to Toddlers
Everything Is Easier When Your Child's Senses Are Happy!
by Britt Collins, MS, OTR/L, and Jackie Olson

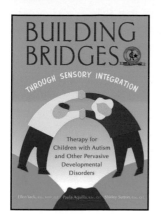

Building Bridges through Sensory Integration

Therapy for Children with Autism and Other Pervasive Developmental Disorders
by Paula Aquilla, Shirley Sutton, and Ellen Yack

Eyegames: Easy and Fun Visual Exercises
An OT and Optometrist Offer Activities to Improve Vision!
by Lois Hickman and Rebecca Hutchins

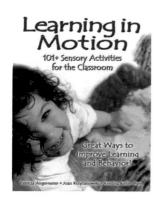

Learning in Motion
101+ Sensory Activities for the Classroom
by Patricia Angermeier, Joan Krzyzanowski, and Kristina Keller Moir

SONGAMES

Each Songame™ CD contains fun musical activities for improving fine- and gross-motor skills, muscle strength, and rhythmicity. These musical gems are useful for engaging kids in active games, as well as helping kids calm down and focus. Songames are great for enhancing oral-motor skills and expressive language play and decreasing tactile, auditory, visual, and sensory defensiveness. Kids will want to play Songames over and over again!

Danceland
Songames™ and Activities to Improve Sensory Skills
by Kristen Fitz Taylor, RPT, and Cheryl McDonald, RPT

Songames™ for Sensory Processing
25 Therapist-Created Musical Activities for Improving Fine & Gross-Motor Skills, Muscle Strength and Rhythmicity
by Aubrey Lande, MS, OTR, Bob Wiz & friends

Marvelous Mouth Music
Songames™ for Speech Development
by Suzanne Evans Morris, PhD, CCC-SLP

28 Instant Songames™
Fun-Filled Activities for Kids 3-8
by Barbara Sher, MS, OTR